BOB DYLAN

THE
VERYBEST

Copyright © 1993 by Special Rider Music
Published by Amsco Publications,
A Division of Music Sales Corporation, New York

Order No. AM 91472
US International Standard Book Number: 0.8256.1376.0
UK International Standard Book Number: 0.7119.3709.5

EXCLUSIVE DISTRIBUTORS:
Music Sales Corporation
257 Park Avenue South, New York, New York 10010 USA
Music Sales Limited
8/9 Frith Street, London W1V 5TZ England
Music Sales Pty. Limited
120 Rothschild Street, Rosebery, Sydney, NSW 2018, Australia

Printed and bound in the United States of America by
Vicks Lithograph and Printing Corporation

Contents

Absolutely Sweet Marie

Words and Music by Bob Dylan

Moderately, with a beat

All Along The Watchtower

Words and Music by Bob Dylan

All I Really Want To Do

Words and Music by Bob Dylan

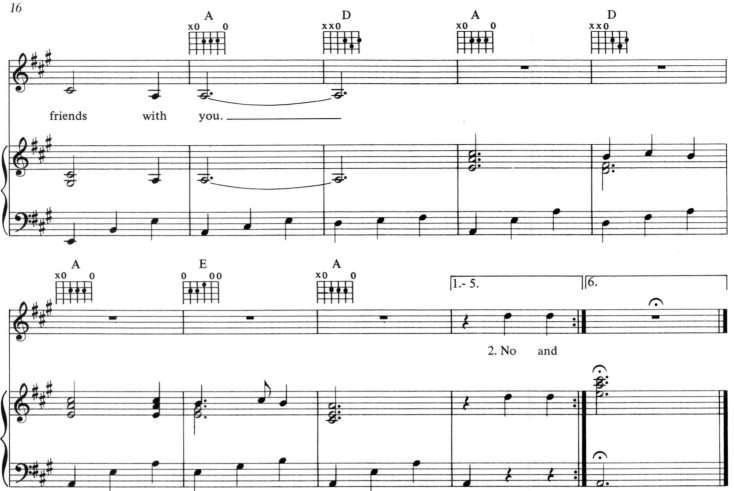

friends   with   you. _____

Additional Lyrics

3. I ain't lookin' to block you up,
   Shock or knock or lock you up,
   Analyze you, categorize you,
   Finalize you or advertise you.
   Chorus

4. I don't want to straight-face you,
   Race or chase you, track or trace you,
   Or disgrace you, or displace you,
   Or define you, or confine you.
   Chorus

5. I don't want to meet your kin,
   Make you spin, or do you in,
   Or select you, or dissect you,
   Or inspect you, or reject you.
   Chorus

6. I don't want to fake you out,
   Take or shake or forsake you out,
   I ain't lookin' for you to feel like me,
   See like me, or be like me.
   Chorus

Blowin' In The Wind

Words and Music by Bob Dylan

friend, is blow-in' in the wind, The an - swer is

blow -in' in the wind.

1.2.   3.

Additional Lyrics

3. How many years can a mountain exist
   before it is washed to the sea?
   Yes 'n' how many years can some people exist
   before they're allowed to be free?
   Yes 'n' how many times can a man turn his head
   pretending that he just doesn't see?

   The answer, my friend, is blowin' in the wind,
   The answer is blowin' in the wind.

Don't Think Twice, It's All Right

Words and Music by Bob Dylan

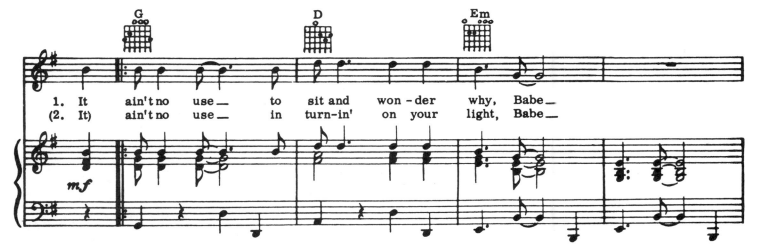

now. / road. When the roost-er / Still I wish there was some-thin' you would do or crows at the break of

dawn / say Look out your win-dow and _____ I'll / To try and make me change my _____ mind and be gone. / stay.

You're the rea-son I'm trav-'lin' on / We nev-er did too_ much talk-in' an-y - way Don't think / So don't think

twice, it's all right. 2. It right. 3. I'm (4. It)

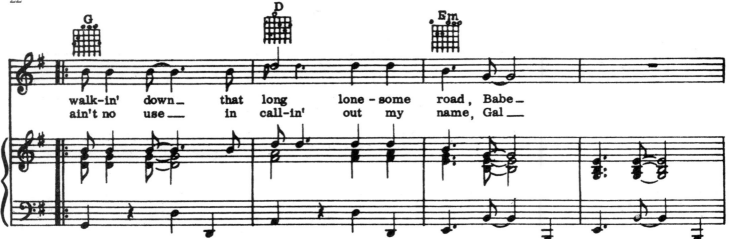

walk-in' down___ that long lone-some road, Babe___
ain't no use___ in call-in' out my name, Gal___

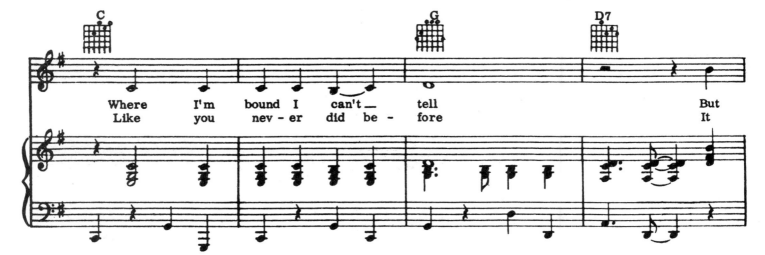

Where I'm bound I can't___ tell
Like you nev-er did be-fore
But
It

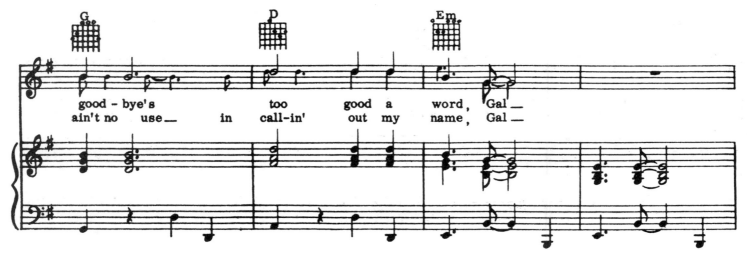

good-bye's too good a word, Gal___
ain't no use___ in call-in' out my name, Gal___

So I'll just say fare thee well.
I can't hear you an-y more.
I ain't
I'm a-

say - in'   you   treat - ed   me   un - kind   You
think - in' and   a - won-d'rin' all   the   way   down the   road   I

could have   done   bet - ter _____ but   I   don't   mind.
once   loved a   wom - an _____ a   child I'm   told.   I

You just kind-a   wast - ed   my pre - cious   time.   But don't think
give   her my   heart but she want - ed   my   soul.   But don't think

twice,   It's all   right.   4. It
twice,   It's all   right.   right.

Gotta Serve Somebody

Words and Music by Bob Dylan

it may be the dev-il or__ it__ may be the Lord. But you're gon-na have to

serve some-bod-y.   2. You

repeat and fade

Additional Lyrics

2. You might be a rock'n'roll addict prancing on the stage.
   You might have drugs at your command, women in a cage.
   You may be a businessman or some high degree thief
   They may call you doctor, or they may call you chief.
   Chorus

3. You may be a state trooper, you might be a young Turk.
   You might be the head of some big TV network.
   You may be rich or poor, you may be blind or lame.
   You may be leaving in another country under another name.
   Chorus

4. You may be a construction worker working on a home.
   You may be living in a mansion, or you might live in a dome.
   You might own guns and you might even own tanks.
   You might be somebody's landlord, you might even own banks.
   Chorus

5. You may be a preacher with your spiritual pride.
   You may be a city councilman taking bribes on the side.
   You may be workin' in a barbershop, you may know how to cut hair.
   You may be somebody's mistress, may be somebody's heir.
   Chorus

6. Might like to wear cotton, might like to wear silk.
   Might like to drink whiskey, might like to drink milk.
   You might like to eat caviar, you might like to eat bread.
   You may be sleeping on the floor, sleeping in a king-sized bed.
   Chorus

7. You may call me Terry, you may call me Timmy.
   You may call me Bobby, you may call me Zimmy.
   You may call me R.J., you may call me Ray.
   You may call me anything, but no matter what you say.
   Chorus

A Hard Rain's A-Gonna Fall

Words and Music by Bob Dylan

Oh, where have you been, my blue-eyed son? Oh,

where have you been, my dar-ling young one? 1. I've

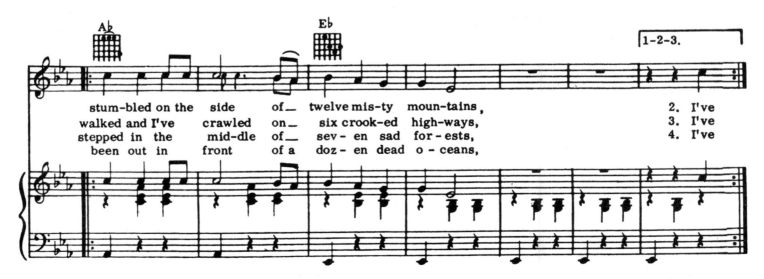

stum-bled on the side of_ twelve mis-ty moun-tains, 2. I've
walked and I've crawled on_ six crook-ed high-ways, 3. I've
stepped in the mid-dle of_ sev-en sad for-ests, 4. I've
been out in front of a doz-en dead o-ceans,

5. I've been ten thou-sand miles in the mouth of a grave-yard,

And it's a hard, and it's a hard, it's a

hard, and it's a hard, and it's a hard rain's _____

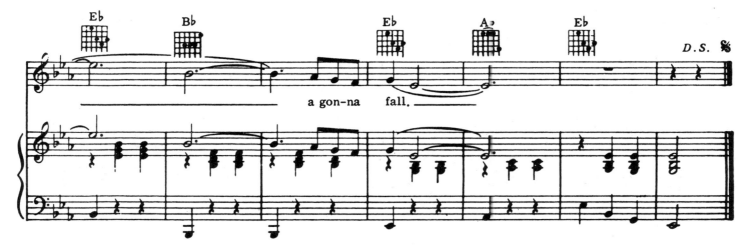

_____ a gon-na fall. _____

D.S.

(A) Oh, what did you see, my blue eyed son?
     Oh, what did you see, my darling young one?

(B) I saw a new born baby with wild wolves all around it,
     I saw a highway of diamonds with nobody on it,
     I saw a black branch with blood that kept drippin',
     I saw a room full of men with their hammers a-bleedin',
     I saw a white ladder all covered with water.
     I saw ten thousand talkers whose tongues were all broken,

(C) I saw guns and sharp swords in the hands of young children,
     And it's a hard, and it's a hard, it's a hard, it's a hard,
     And it's a hard rain's a gonna fall.

(A) And what did you hear, my blue eyed son?
     And what did you hear, my darling young one?

(B) I heard the sound of a thunder, it roared out a warnin',
     Heard the roar of a wave that could drown the whole world,
     Heard one hundred drummers whose hands were a blazin',
     Heard ten thousand whisperin' and nobody listenin',
     Heard one person starve, I heard many people laughin',
     Heard the song of a poet who died in the gutter,

(C) Heard the sound of a clown who cried in the alley,
     And it's a hard, and it's a hard, it's a hard, it's a hard
     And it's a hard rain's a gonna fall.

(A) Oh, who did you meet, my blue eyed son?
     Who did you meet, my darling young one?

(B) I met a young child beside a dead pony,
     I met a white man who walked a black dog,
     I met a woman whose body was burning,
     I met a young girl, she gave me a rainbow,
     I met one man who was wounded in love,

(C) I met another man who was wounded with hatred,
     And it's a hard, it's a hard, it's a hard, it's a hard
     It's a hard rain's a gonna fall.

(A) Oh, what'll you do now, my blue eyed son?
     Oh, what'll you do now, my darling young one?

(B) I'm a goin' back out 'fore the rain starts a fallin',
     I'll walk to the depth of the deepest black forest,
     Where the people are many and their hands are all empty,
     Where the pellets of poison are flooding their waters,
     Where the home in the valley meets the damp dirty prison,
     Where the executioner's face is always well hidden,
     Where hunger is ugly, where souls are forgotten,
     Where black is the color, where none is the number,
     And I'll tell it and think it and speak it and breathe it,
     And reflect it from the mountain so all souls can see it,
     Then I'll stand on the ocean until I start sinkin',

(C) But I'll know my song well before I start singin',
     And it's a hard, it's a hard, it's a hard, it's a hard,
     It's a hard rain's a gonna fall.

I Shall Be Released

Words and Music by Bob Dylan

Moderately

Additional Lyrics

2. Down here next to me in this lonely crowd
   Is a man who swears he's not to blame.
   All day long I hear him cry so loud,
   Calling out that he's been framed.

   Chorus

3. They say ev'rything can be replaced,
   Yet ev'ry distance is not near.
   So I remember ev'ry face
   Of ev'ry man who put me here.

   Chorus

I Want You

Words and Music by Bob Dylan

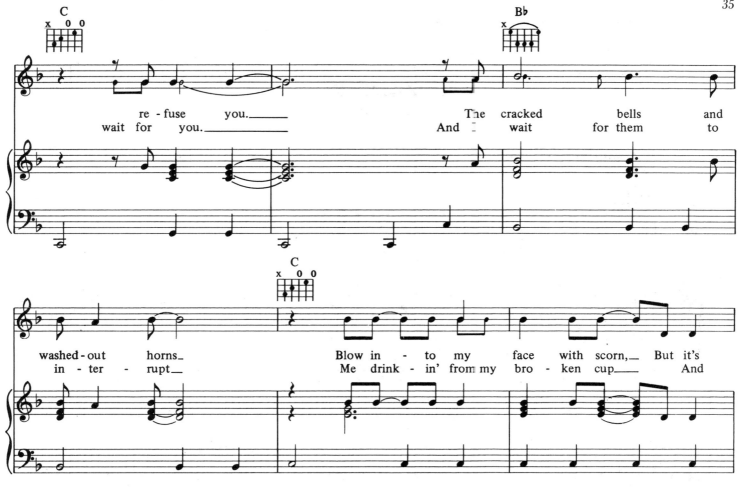

re-fuse you._____
wait for you._____

The cracked bells and
And I wait for them to

washed-out horns__
in-ter-rupt__

Blow in-to my face with scorn,__ But it's
Me drink-in' from my bro-ken cup__ And

not that way, I was-n't born__ to lose you._____
ask me__ to o-pen up__ the gate for you._____

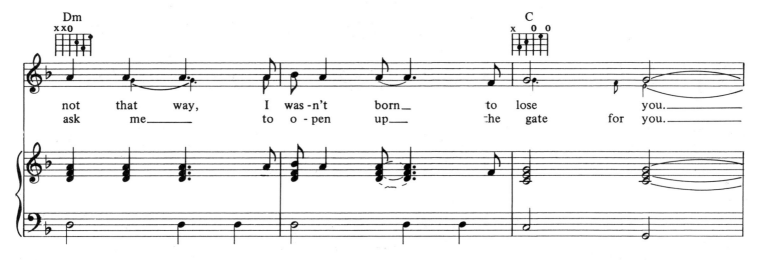

Chorus:

I want you,   I

Interlude:

all my fa-thers, they've gone down,_ True love they've_ been with-

out it. But all their daugh-ters put me down 'Cause I don't think a-bout_

_ it. 3. Well, I re-

D.S.al Fine
(3rd and 4th Verses)

Additional Lyrics

3. Well, I return to the Queen of Spades
   And talk with my chambermaid.
   She knows that I'm not afraid
   To look at her.
   She is good to me,
   And there's nothing she doesn't see.
   She knows where I'd like to be,
   But it doesn't matter.
   Chorus

4. Now your dancing child with his Chinese suit,
   He spoke to me, I took his flute.
   No, I wasn't very cute to him,
   Was I?
   But I did it, though, because he lied,
   Because he took you for a ride,
   And because time was on his side,
   And because I ...
   Chorus

I'll Be Your Baby Tonight

Words and Music by Bob Dylan

shoes off,___ Do not fear,___ Bring that bot-

-tle o-ver here,___

I'll ___ be your ___ ba-by to-

night. ___

It Ain't Me, Babe

Words and Music by Bob Dylan

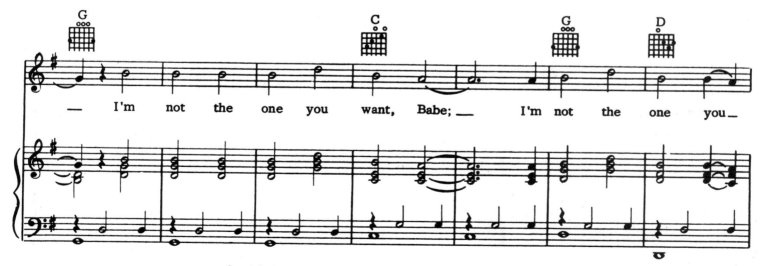

need. _____ You say you're work-in' for some - one__ nev-er

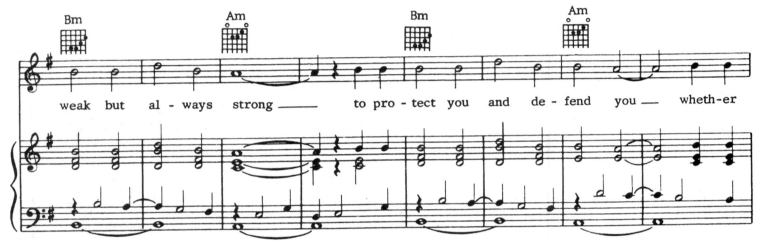

weak but al - ways strong _____ to pro - tect you and de - fend you __ wheth-er

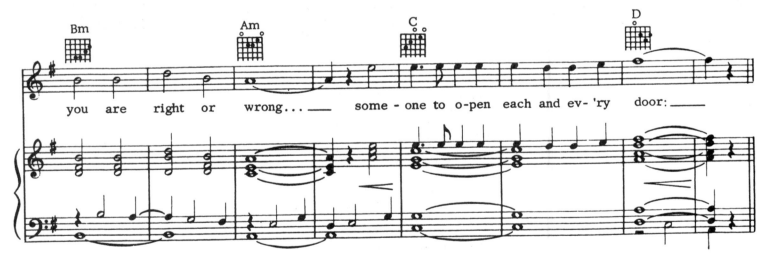

you are right or wrong... __ some - one to o-pen each and ev-'ry door: ____

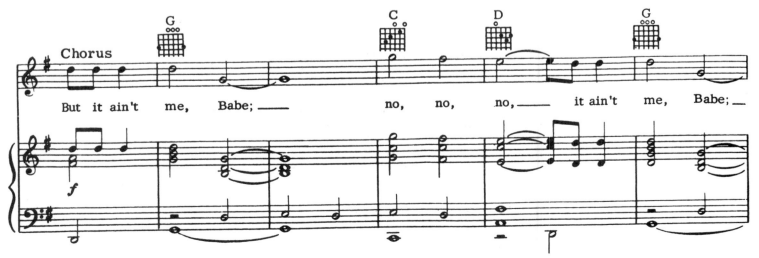

Chorus

But it ain't me, Babe; ___ no, no, no, ___ it ain't me, Babe; __

It ain't me you're look - in' for, Babe.

2. Go lightly from the ledge Babe,
Go lightly on the ground,
I'm not the one you want, Babe,
I will only let you down.
You say you're looking for someone
Who will promise never to part,
Someone to close his eyes for you,
Someone to close his heart.
Someone who will die for you an' more
But it ain't me, Babe,
No, no, no it ain't me, Babe,
It ain't me you're looking for, Babe.

3. Go melt back into the nite Babe,
Everything inside is made of stone,
There's nothing in here moving
An' anyway I'm not alone.
You say you're looking for someone
Who'll pick you up each time you fall,
To gather flowers constantly
An' to come each time you call.
A lover for your life an' nothing more
But it ain't me, Babe,
No, no, no it ain't me, Babe,
It ain't me you're looking for, Babe.

If Not For You

Words and Music by Bob Dylan

be no-where at all. Oh! — What would I — do, — If not — for you. —

If not for you, —

Win-ter would

Just Like A Woman

Words and Music by Bob Dylan

Knockin' On Heaven's Door

Words and Music by Bob Dylan

Lay, Lady, Lay

Words and Music by Bob Dylan

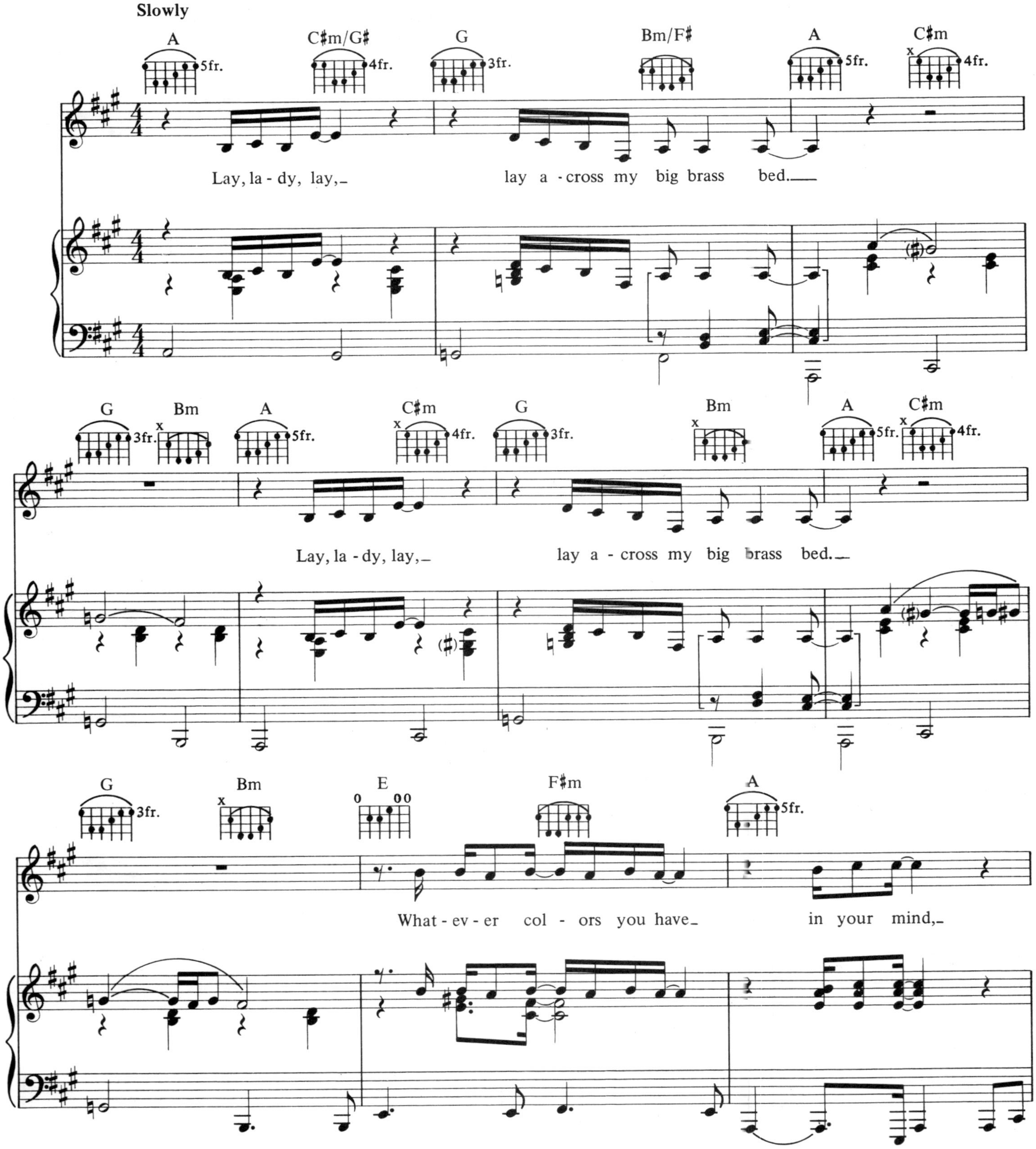

I'll show them to you and you'll see them shine.— Lay, la - dy, lay,—

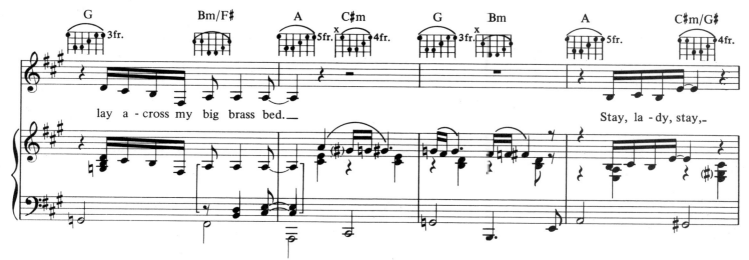

lay a - cross my big brass bed.— Stay, la - dy, stay,—

stay with your man_ a - while.— Un - til the break of_ day,—

let me see you make him smile.—

You can have your cake___ and eat it too.___

Why wait an-y long-er for___ the one you love,___ When he's stand-

-ing in front of you.___

Lay, la-dy, lay,___

lay a-cross my big brass bed.___

Stay, la-dy, stay,___

Maggie's Farm

Words and Music by Bob Dylan

Medium bright

FARM no more ___ Well I wake in the

morn-ing Fold my hands and pray for rain. I got a head full of i-

de-as ___ That are driv-in' me in-sane ___ It's a shame the way she

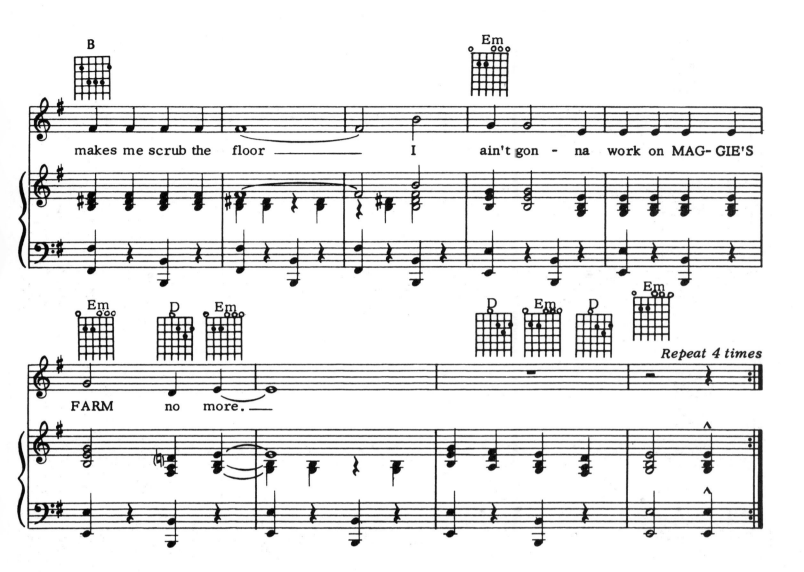

Repeat 4 times

makes me scrub the floor _____ I ain't gon - na work on MAG- GIE'S

FARM no more. _____

2. I ain't gonna work for Maggie's brother no more
   No, I ain't gonna work for Maggie's brother no more
   Well he hands you a nickel
   He hands you a dime
   He asks with a grin
   If you're havin' a good time
   Then he fines you every time you slam the door
   I ain't gonna work for Maggie's brother no more.

3. I ain't gonna work for Maggie's pa no more
   No, I ain't gonna work for Maggie's pa no more
   Well he puts his cigar
   Out in your face just for kicks
   His bedroom window
   It is made out of bricks
   The National Guard stands around his door
   Ah, I ain't gonna work for Maggie's pa no more.

4. I ain't gonna work for Maggie's ma no more
   No, I ain't gonna work for Maggie's ma no more
   Well she talks to all the servants
   About man and God and law
   Everybody says she's the brains behind pa
   She's sixty-eight, but she says she's twenty-four
   I ain't gonna work for Maggie's ma no more.

5. I ain't gonna work on Maggie's farm no more
   I ain't gonna work on Maggie's farm no more
   Well, I try my best
   To be just like I am
   But everybody wants you
   To be just like them
   They sing while you slave
   And I just get bored
   I ain't gonna work on Maggie's farm no more.

Like A Rolling Stone

Words and Music by Bob Dylan

Once up-on__ a time you dressed so fine,__ You threw the bums a dime

in your prime, __ Did - n't you?__

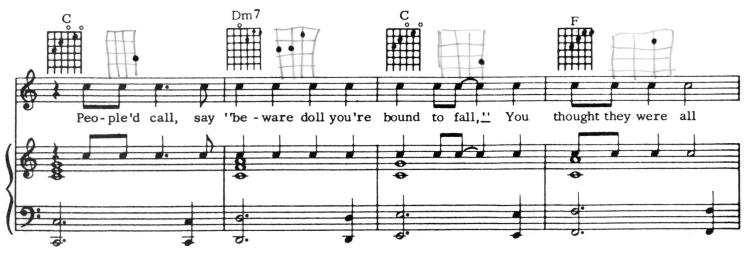

Peo-ple'd call, say "be-ware doll you're bound to fall," You thought they were all

kid - din' you._ You used to

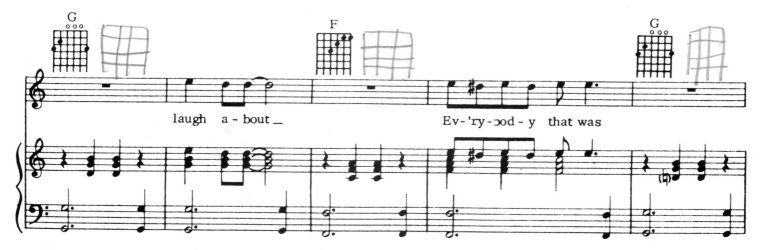

laugh a - bout _ Ev - 'ry - bod - y that was

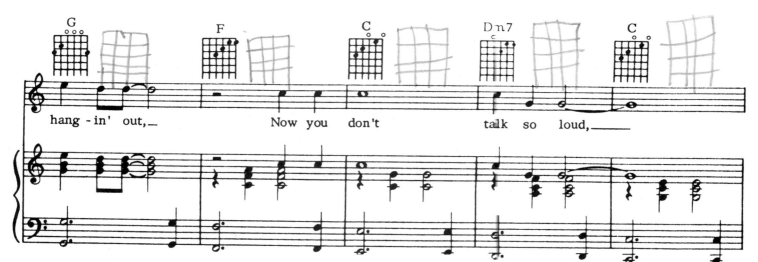

hang - in' out,_ Now you don't talk so loud,_____

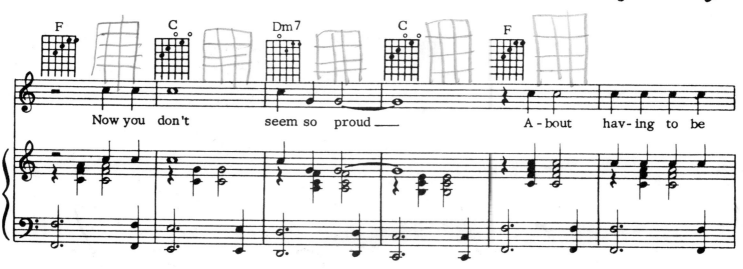

Now you don't seem so proud _____ A - bout hav - ing to be

scroung - ing for your next meal.

Refrain

How does it feel, How does it feel,

To be with-out a home,

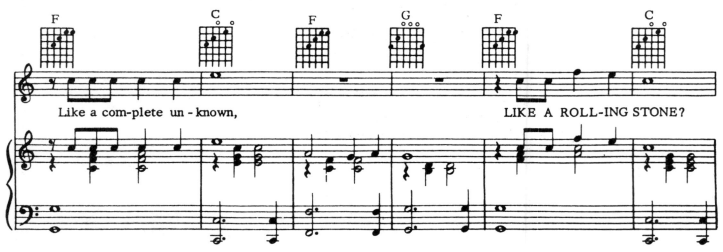

Like a com-plete un - known, LIKE A ROLL-ING STONE?

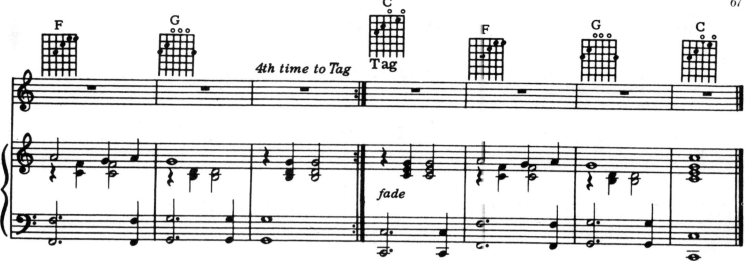

Verse 2. You've gone to the finest school all right Miss Lonely,
But you know you only used to get
Juiced in it.
And nobody's ever taught you how to live on the street
And now you're gonna have to get
Used to it.
You said you'd never compromise
With the mystery tramp, but now you realize
He's not selling any alibis
As you stare into the vacuum of his eyes
And ask him do you want to
Make a deal?

Refrain:

Verse 3. You never turned around to see the frowns on the jugglers and the clowns
When they all come down
And did tricks for you
You never understood that it ain't no good
You shouldn't let other people
Get your kicks for you.
You used to ride on the chrome horse with your diplomat
Who carried on his shoulder a Siamese cat,
Ain't it hard when you discovered that
He really wasn't where it's at
After he took from you everything
He could steal.

Refrain:

Verse 4. Princess on the steeple
And all the pretty people're drinkin', thinkin'
That they got it made.
Exchanging all kinds of precious gifts and things
But you'd better lift your diamond ring,
You'd better pawn it babe,
You used to be so amused
At Napoleon in rags and the language that he used
Go to him now, he calls you, you can't refuse
When you got nothing,you got nothing to lose,
You're invisible now, you got no secrets
To conceal.

Refrain:

Masters Of War

Words and Music by Bob Dylan

walls   You that hide be-hind desks   I just

want you to know I can see through your masks   *D.S.* %

2. You that never done nothin'
   But build to destroy
   You play with my world
   Like it's your little toy
   You put a gun in my hand
   And you hide from my eyes
   And you turn and run farther
   When the fast bullets fly

3. Like Judas of old
   You lie and deceive
   A world war can be won
   You want me to believe
   But I see through your eyes
   And I see through your brain
   Like I see through the water
   That runs down my drain

4. You fasten the triggers
   For the others to fire
   Then you set back and watch
   When the death count gets higher
   You hide in your mansion
   As young people's blood
   Flows out of their bodies
   And is buried in the mud

5. You've thrown the worst fear
   That can ever be hurled
   Fear to bring children
   Into the world
   For threatenin' my baby
   Unborn and unnamed
   You ain't worth the blood
   That runs in your veins

6. How much do I know
   To talk out of turn
   You might say that I'm young
   You might say I'm unlearned
   But there's one thing I know
   Though I'm younger than you
   Even Jesus would never
   Forgive what you do

7. Let me ask you one question
   Is your money that good
   Will it buy you forgiveness
   Do you think that it could
   I think you will find
   When your death takes its toll
   All the money you made
   Will never buy back your soul

8. And I hope that you die
   And your death'll come soon
   I will follow your casket
   On a pale afternoon
   And I'll watch while you're lowered
   Down to your death bed
   And I'll stand o'er your grave
   Till I'm sure that you're dead.

Mr. Tambourine Man

Words and Music by Bob Dylan

Repeat 3 times

brand - ed on my feet. I have no one to meet And the

an - cient emp - ty street's too dead for dream-in'. _____

Refrain:

Verse 2. Take me on a trip upon your magic swirlin' ship
My senses have been stripped, my hands can't feel to grip
My toes too numb to step, wait only for my boot heels
To be wanderin'
I'm ready to go anywhere, I'm ready for to fade
Into my own parade, cast your dancin' spell my way
I promise to go under it.

Refrain:

Verse 3. Though you might hear laughin' spinnin' swingin' madly across the sun
It's not aimed at anyone, it's just escapin' on the run
And but for the sky there are no fences facin'
And if you hear vague traces of skippin' reels of rhyme
To your tambourine in time, it's just a ragged clown behind
I wouldn't pay it any mind, it's just a shadow you're
Seein' that he's chasin'.

Refrain:

Verse 4. Then take me disappearin' through the smoke rings of my mind
Down the foggy ruins of time, far past the frozen leaves
The haunted, frightened trees out to the windy beach
Far from the twisted reach of crazy sorrow
Yes, to dance beneath the diamond sky with one hand wavin' free
Silhouetted by the sea, circled by the circus sands
With all memory and fate driven deep beneath the waves
Let me forget about today until tomorrow.

Refrain:

Quinn The Eskimo
(The Mighty Quinn)

Words and Music by Bob Dylan

Moderately slow, with a steady beat

Come all with-out, Come on with-in, You'll

not see noth-in' like the might-y Quinn.

might-y Quinn.

Additional Lyrics

2. I like to do just like the rest,
   I like my sugar sweet,
   But guarding fumes and making haste,
   It ain't my cup of meat.
   Ev'rybody's 'neath the trees feeding pigeons on a limb,
   But when Quinn, the eskimo gets here,
   All the pigeons gonna run to him.
   Chorus

3. A cat's meown, and a cow's moo,
   I can't recite them all.
   Just Tell me where it hurts yuh, honey,
   And I'll tell you who to call.
   Nobody can get no sleep, there's someone on ev'rone's toes,
   But when the eskimo gets here,
   Ev'rybody's gonna want to doze.
   Chorus

Political World

Words and Music by Bob Dylan

don't have a face.___ 2.We

live in a po-lit-i-cal world,___ I-ci-cles hang-ing down,___

Wed-ding bells ring and an-gels sing,___ Clouds___ cov-er up the ground.___

3. We

live in a po-lit-i-cal world,__ Wis-dom is thrown in-to jail,__ It

rots in a cell, is mis-guid-ed as hell, Leav-ing no one to pick up a trail.__

Gm

4. We

Gomit3rd
x 0 0

live in a po-lit-i-cal world__ Where mer-cy walks the plank,__

Life is in mir - rors, death dis - ap - pears Up the steps in - to the near - est bank.

Gm

1. 2.

5. We

Gomit3rd
x 0 0

live in a po - lit - i - cal world Where cour - age is a thing of the past,

Hous - es are haunt - ed, chil - dren are un - want - ed, The next day could be your last.

6. We

live in a po-lit-i-cal world,_ The one we can see and can feel._ But there's

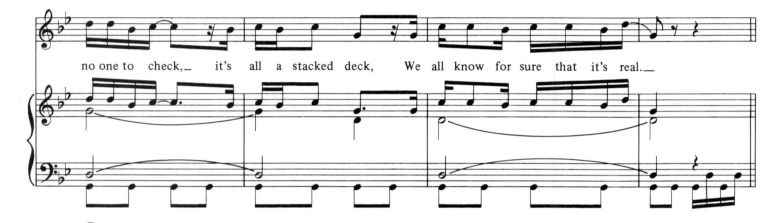

no one to check,_ it's all a stacked deck, We all know for sure that it's real._

Gm

7. We

Gomit3rd
x00

live in a po-lit-i-cal world,_ In the cit-ies of lone-some fear._

Lit - tle by lit - tle you turn in the mid - dle, But you're nev - er sure why you're here.___ 8. We

live in a po - lit - i - cal world,___ Un - der the mi - cro - scope,___ You can

trav - el an - y - where and hang___ your - self there, You al - ways got more than e - nough rope.

Gm

9. We

Gomit3rd
x00

live in a po-lit-i-cal world,_ Turn-ing and a-thrash-ing a-bout._ As

soon as you're a-wake, you're trained_ to take_ What looks like the eas-y way out._

Gm

10. We

Gomit3rd
x00

live in a po-lit-i-cal world_ Where peace is not wel-come at all, ___ It's turned a-

way from the door_ to wan-der some more_ Or put up a-gainst the wall._ 11. We

live in a po-lit-i-cal world,_ Ev-ery-thing is hers_ or his,_

Climb in-to the frame and shout_ God's name, But you're nev-er sure what it is.___

Gm

Repeat and fade

Rainy Day Women #12 & 35

Words and Music by Bob Dylan

Moderately (in 2)

1. Well, they'll stone ya when you're try'n' to be so good, _____ They'll stone ya just-a like they said they would. _____ They'll

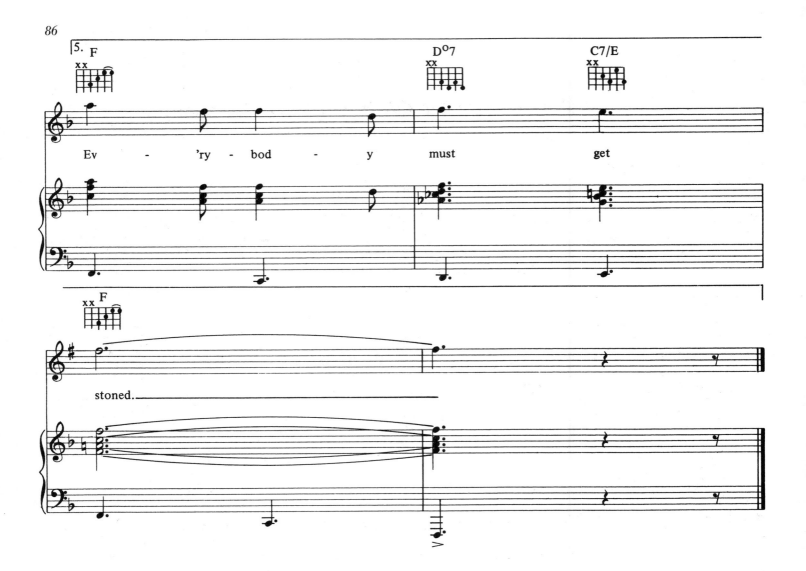

Additional Lyrics

2. Well, they'll stone ya when you're walkin' 'long the street.
They'll stone ya when you're tryin' to keep your seat.
They'll stone ya when you're walkin' on the floor.
They'll stone ya when you're walkin' to the door.
But I would not feel so all alone,
Everybody must get stoned.

3. They'll stone ya when you're at the breakfast table.
They'll stone ya when you are young and able.
They'll stone ya when you're tryin' to make a buck.
They'll stone ya and then they'll say, "Good luck."
Tell ya what, I would not feel so all alone,
Everybody must get stoned.

4. Well, they'll stone you and say that it's the end.
Then they'll stone you and then they'll come back again.
They'll stone you when you're riding in your car.
They'll stone you when you're playing your guitar.
Yes, but I would not feel so all alone,
Everybody must get stoned.

5. Well, they'll stone you when you walk all alone.
They'll stone you when you are walking home.
They'll stone you and then say you are brave.
They'll stone you when you are set down in your grave.
But I would not feel so all alone,
Everybody must get stoned.

Sad Eyed Lady Of The Lowlands

Words and Music by Bob Dylan

wait?___

2. With your

Additional Lyrics

2. With your sheets like metal and your belt like lace,
   And your deck of cards missing the jack and the ace,
   And your basement clothes and your hollow face,
   Who among them can think he could outguess you?
   With your silhouette when the sunlight dims
   Into your eyes where the moonlight swims,
   And your match-book songs and your gypsy hymns,
   Who among them would try to impress you?
   Chorus

3. The kings of Tyrus with their convict list
   Are waiting in line for their geranium kiss,
   And you wouldn't know it would happen like this,
   But who among them really wants just to kiss you?
   With your childhood flames on your midnight rug,
   And your Spanish manners and your mother's drugs,
   And your cowboy mouth and your curfew plugs,
   Who among them do you think could resist you"
   Chorus

4. Oh, the farmers and the businessmen, they all did decide
   To show you the dead angels that they used to hide.
   But why did they pick you to sympathize with their side?
   Oh, how could they ever mistake you?
   They wished you'd accepted the blame for the farm,
   But with the sea at your feet and the phony false alarm,
   And with the child of a hoodlum wrapped up in your arms,
   How could they ever, ever persuade you?
   Chorus

5. With your sheet-metal memory of Cannery Row,
   And your magazine-husband who one day just had to go,
   And your gentleness now which you just can't help but show,
   Who among them do you think would employ you?
   Now you stand with your thief, you're on his parole
   With your holy medallion which your fingertips fold,
   And your saintlike face and your ghostlike soul,
   Oh, who among them do you think could destroy you?
   Chorus

Stuck Inside of Mobile With the Memphis Blues Again

Words and Music by Bob Dylan

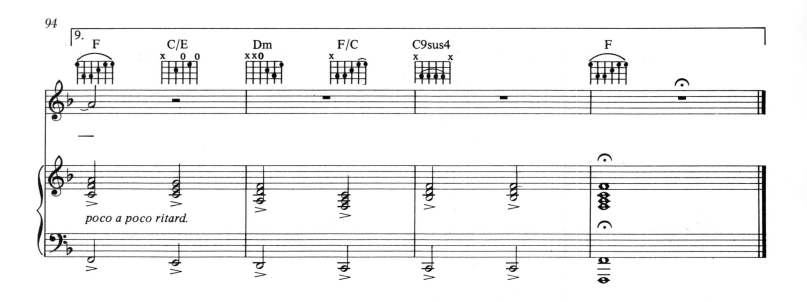

poco a poco ritard.

Additional Lyrics

2. Well, Shakespeare, he's in the alley
   With his pointed shoes and his bells,
   Speaking to some French girl
   Who says she knows me well.
   And I would send a message
   To find out if she's talked,
   But the post office has been stolen
   And the mailbox is locked.
   Chorus

3. Mona tried to tell me
   To stay away from the train line.
   She said that all the railroad men
   Just drink up your blood like wine.
   An' I said, "Oh, I didn't know that,
   But then again, there's only one I've met,
   An' he just smoked my eyelids
   An' punched my cigarette."
   Chorus

4. Grandpa died last week
   And now he's buried in the rocks,
   But everybody still talks about
   How badly they were shocked.
   But me, I expected it to happen,
   I knew he'd lost control
   When he built a fire on Main Street
   And shot it full of holes.
   Chorus

5. Now the senator came down here
   Showing ev'ryone his gun,
   Handing out free tickets
   To the wedding of his son.
   An' me, I nearly got busted,
   An' wouldn't it be my luck
   To get caught without a ticket
   And be discovered beneath a truck.
   Chorus

6. Now the preacher looked so baffled
   When I asked him why he dressed
   With twenty pounds of headlines
   Stapled to his chest.
   But he cursed me when I proved it to him,
   Then I whispered, "Not even you can hide.
   You see, you're just like me,
   I hope you're satisfied."
   Chorus

7. Now the rainman gave me two cures,
   Then he said, "Jump right in."
   The one was Texas medicine,
   The other was just railroad gin.
   An' like a fool I mixed them,
   An' it strangled up my mind.
   An' now people just get uglier,
   An' I have no sense of time.
   Chorus

8. When Ruthie says come see her
   In her honky-tonk lagoon,
   Where I can watch her waltz for free
   'Neath her Panamanian moon,
   An' I say, "Aw come on now,
   You must know about my debutante."
   An' she says, "Your debutante just knows what you need,
   But I know what you want."
   Chorus

9. Now the bricks lay on Grand Street
   Where the neon madmen climb.
   They all fall there so perfectly,
   It all seems so well timed.
   An' here I sit so patiently,
   Waiting to find out what price,
   You have to pay to get out of
   Going through all these things twice.
   Chorus

Tonight I'll Be Staying Here With You

Words and Music by Bob Dylan

Throw my suit-case out _ there, too,

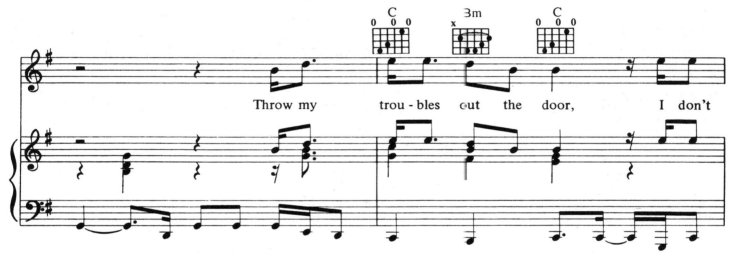

Throw my trou-bles out the door, I don't

need them an-y more 'Cause to-night I'll be stay-ing here with you.

Subterranean Homesick Blues

Words and Music by Bob Dylan

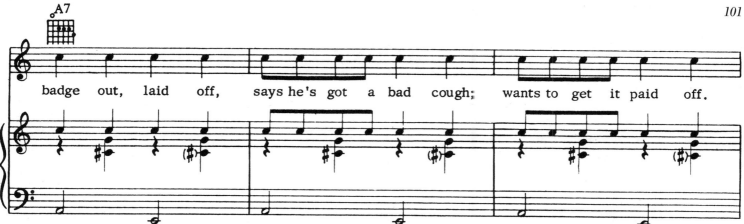

badge out, laid off, says he's got a bad cough; wants to get it paid off.

Look out, kid,— it's some-thin' you did;— God knows when,—but you're

do - in' it a - gain! You bet - ter duck down the al - ley-way

look-in' for a new friend; the man in the coon - skin cap by the big pen

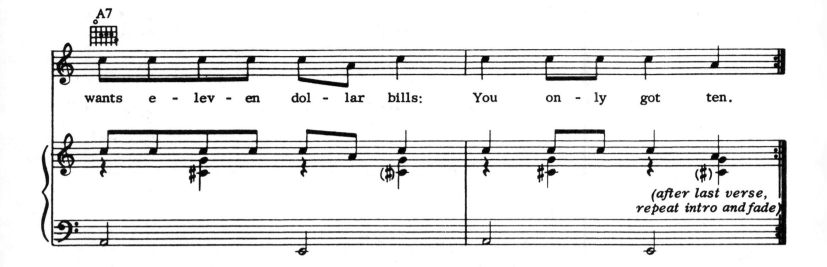

wants e - lev - en dol - lar bills: You on - ly got ten.

(after last verse, repeat intro and fade)

2. Maggie comes fleet foot
Face full of black soot
Talkin' at the heat put
Plants in the bed but
The phone's tapped any-way
Maggie says that many say
They must bust in early May
Orders from the D. A.
Look out kid
Don't matter what you did
Walk on your tip toes
Don't try "No Doz"
Better stay away from those
That carry around a fire hose
Keep a clean nose
Watch the plain clothes
You don't need a weather man
To know which way the wind blows.

3. Get sick, get well
Hang around a ink well
Ring bell, hard to tell
If anything is goin' to sell
Try hard, get barred
Get back, write braille
Get jailed, jump bail
Join the army, if you fail
Look out kid, you're gonna get hit
But users, cheaters
Six time losers
Hang around the theatres
Girl by the whirlpool
Lookin' for a new fool
Don't follow leaders
Watch the parkin' meters

4. Ah get born, keep warm
Short pants, romance, learn to dance
Get dressed, get blessed
Try to be a success
Please her, please him, buy gifts
Don't steal, don't lift
Twenty years of schoolin'
And they put you on the day shift
Look out kid they keep it all hid
Better jump down a manhole
Light yourself a candle, don't wear sandals
Try to avoid the scandals
Don't wanna be a bum
You better chew gum
The pump don't work
'cause the vandals took the handles.

When I Paint My Masterpiece

Words and Music by Bob Dylan

Tangled up in Blue

Words and Music by Bob Dylan

Additional Lyrics

2. She was married when we first met,
   Soon to be divorced.
   I helped her out of a jam, I guess,
   But I used a little too much force.
   We drove that car as far as we could,
   Abandoned it out West.
   Split up on a dark sad night,
   Both agreeing it was best.
   She turned around to look at me,
   As I was walkin' away.
   I heard her say over my shoulder,
   "We'll meet again some day
   on the avenue."
   Tangled up in blue.

3. I had a job in the great north woods,
   Working as a cook for a spell.
   But I never did like it all that much,
   And one day the axe just fell.
   So I drifted down to New Orleans,
   Where I happened to be employed.
   Workin' for a while on a fishin' boat,
   Right outside of Delacroix.
   But all the while I was alone,
   The past was close behind.
   I seen a lot of women,
   But she never escaped my mind,
   And I just grew.
   Tangled up in blue.

4. She was workin' in a topless place,
   And I stopped in for a beer.
   I just kept lookin' at the side of her face,
   In the spotlight so clear.
   And later on as the crowd thinned out,
   I's just about to do the same.
   She was standing there in back of my chair,
   Said to me, "Don't I know your name?"
   I muttered somethin' underneath my breath,
   She studied the lines on my face.
   I must admit I felt a little uneasy,
   When she bent down to tie the laces
   Of my shoe.
   Tangled up in blue.

5. She lit a burner on the stove,
   And offered me a pipe.
   "I thought you'd never say hello," she said,
   "You look like the silent type."
   Then she opened up a book of poems,
   And handed it to me.
   Written by an Italian poet
   From the thirteenth century.
   And every one of them words rang true,
   And glowed like burnin' coal.
   Pourin' off of every page,
   Like it was written in my soul
   From me to you.
   Tangled up in blue.

6. I lived with them on Montague Street,
   In a basement down the stairs.
   There was music in the cafes at night,
   And revolution in the air.
   Then he started into dealing with slaves,
   And something inside of him died.
   She had to sell everything she owned,
   And froze up inside.
   And when finally the bottom fell out,
   I became withdrawn.
   The only thing I knew how to do,
   Was to keep on keepin' on,
   Like a bird that flew.
   Tangled up in blue.

7. So now I'm goin' back again,
   I got to get to her somehow.
   All the people we used to know,
   They're an illusion to me now.
   Some are mathematicians,
   Some are carpenters' wives.
   Don't know how it all got started,
   I don't know what they're doin' with their lives.
   But me, I'm still on the road,
   Headin' for another joint.
   We always did feel the same,
   We just saw it from a different point
   Of view.
   Tangled up in blue.

The Times They Are A-Changin'

Words and Music by Bob Dylan

2. Come writers and critics
   Who prophecies with your pen
   And keep your eyes wide
   The chance won't come again.
   And don't speak too soon
   For the wheel's still in spin
   And there's no tellin' who
   That it's namin'
   For the loser now
   Will be later to win
   For the times they are a-changin'.

3. Come senators, congressmen
   Please heed the call
   Don't stand in the doorway
   Don't block up the hall.
   For he that gets hurt
   Will be he who has stalled
   There's a battle
   Outside and it's ragin'
   It'll soon shake your windows
   And rattle your walls
   For the times they are a-changin'.

4. Come mothers and fathers,
   Throughout the land
   And don't criticize
   What you can't understand.
   Your sons and your daughters
   Are beyond your command
   Your old road is
   Rapidly agin'
   Please get out of the new one
   If you can't lend your hand
   For the times they are a-changin'.

5. The line it is drawn
   The curse it is cast
   The slow one now will
   Later be fast.
   As the present now
   Will later be past
   The order is rapidly fadin'
   And the first one now
   Will later be last
   For the times they are a-changin'.